21 Pieces For Violin With Guitar

**Selections from
Suzuki™ Violin School,
Vols. 1, 2 and 3
For Violin with Classic Guitar Accompaniments
and Optional Chords for Folk Guitarists**

Arranged by Thomas F. Heck

© 1989 Summy-Birchard Music, division of Summy-Birchard Inc.
exclusively distributed by
Warner Bros. Publications Inc.
Secaucus, New Jersey, U.S.A.
All Right Reserved. Printed in U.S.A.

ISBN 0-87487-295-2
10 9 8 7 6 5 4 3 2
The Suzuki name, logo and wheel device
are trademarks of Summy-Birchard Inc.

FOREWORD

Welcome to an enriching new way to accompany selections from the Suzuki repertoire! The idea of pairing the guitar with the violin on these famous little pieces derives from my own experience as a classic guitarist accompanying my daughter, Larissa, during the late 1970s, when she worked her way successfully through the first five books of the *Suzuki Violin School*.

We found that the guitar provided an interesting and useful alternative to the piano. And whenever there was no piano available (outdoors, or in certain public meeting rooms, for example), the guitar was always called on to provide harmonic and rhythmic support, not only for solos, but also for ensembles and "play-ins." The students loved it!

These guitar accompaniments are based exclusively on the published piano accompaniments to Books 1-3 of the *Suzuki Violin School*. The transcriptions, while simplified for the sake of playability, are fully compatible with their piano models. Both versions may be played together in group situations, as readily as either may stand alone with the solo violin part.

Guitar chords are provided for those who do not read classic guitar notation but would like to strum along or do some kind of "finger pickin'." I hope that all guitarists will familiarize themselves with the tried-and-true piano accompaniments to these pieces, so as to imitate them as best they can.

Many guitarists will also find a "chord finder" book useful in fingering some of the chords found in the more advanced pieces in Books 2 & 3. At times, too, playing the "countermelodies" that occur at certain places, like in the Trio of Beethoven's Minuet in G from Book 2, will be helpful.

As a veteran "Suzuki parent," I trust that this small contribution will enhance the goal of supportive parent-child interaction, which is so important to the success of the Suzuki method. Whatever more the edition may do by way of enriching the repertoire for violin and guitar is gratifying, but secondary to what I consider its main pedagogical and supportive intent.

Thomas F. Heck, Ph.D.
The Ohio State University

ACKNOWLEDGMENT

A special word of thanks is due to the Guitar Committee of the Suzuki Association of the Americas for offering a number of helpful corrections and suggestions.

CONTENTS

		Page	Suzuki™ Violin School
Twinkle, Twinkle Little Star			
Theme	*Folk song*	6	Bk. 1 p. 14
Variations	*S. Suzuki*	7	Bk. 1 p. 15
Song of the Wind	*Folk Song*	8	Bk. 1 p. 16
Go Tell Aunt Rhody	*Folk Song*	8	Bk. 1 p. 17
O Come, Little Children	*Folk song*	9	Bk. 1 p. 17
May Song	*Folk song*	10	Bk. 1 p. 19
Long, Long Ago	*T. H. Bayly*	10	Bk. 1 p. 19
Allegro	*S. Suzuki*	11	Bk. 1 p. 20
Minuet 1, from Suite in G min., BWV 822	*J. S. Bach*	12	Bk. 1 p. 26
Minuet 2, BWV Anh. 116	*J. S. Bach*	12	Bk. 1 p. 27
Minuet 3, BWV Anh. 114	*J. S. Bach*	14	Bk. 1 p. 28
Chorus from "Judas Maccabaeus"	*G. F. Handel*	15	Bk. 2 p. 7
Gavotte	*F. J. Gossec*	16	Bk. 1 p. 30
Musette, Gavotte II from English Suite #3, BWV 808	*J. S. Bach*	17	Bk. 2 p. 7
Waltz, Op. 39, no. 15	*J. Brahms*	18	Bk. 2 p. 10
Theme from "Witches' Dance"	*N. Paganini*	20	Bk. 2 p. 13
Minuet in G	*L. van Beethoven*	22	Bk. 2 p. 18
Minuet, from Quintet in E	*L. Boccherini*	24	Bk. 2 p. 19
Humoresque, Op. 101, no. 7	*A. Dvořák*	26	Bk. 3 p. 14
Gavotte	*P. Martini*	28	Bk. 3 p. 8
Gavotte I and II, from Orchestral Suite in D, BWV 1068	*J.S. Bach*	32	Bk. 3 p. 18
Minuets, from "A Notebook for Anna Magdalena," BWV Anh. 114 & 115	*J.S. Bach*	34	Bk. 3 p. 10

Twinkle, Twinkle, Little Star
Theme

Folk Song

Variations

The accompanying guitarist should play the same rhythmic "variations" in the melody as the violinist. The underlying accompaniment remains the same.

S. Suzuki

Song of the Wind

Folk Song

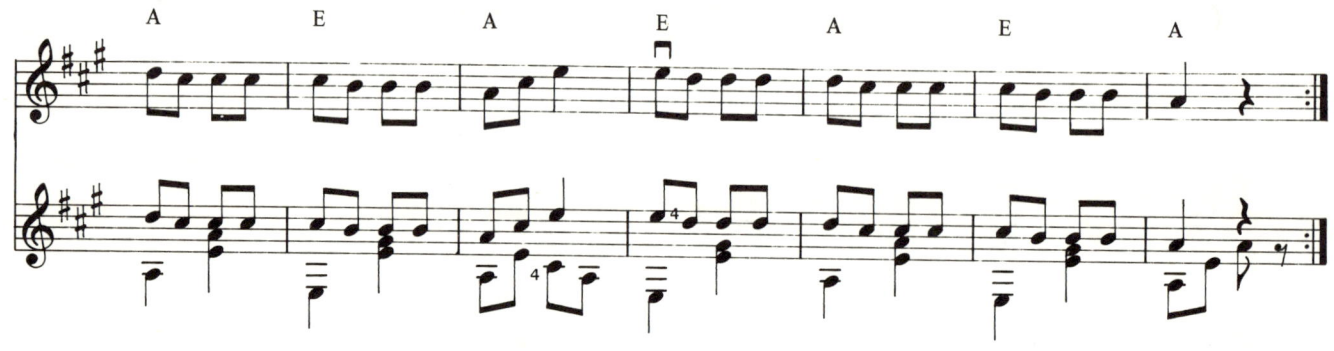

Go Tell Aunt Rhody

Folk Song

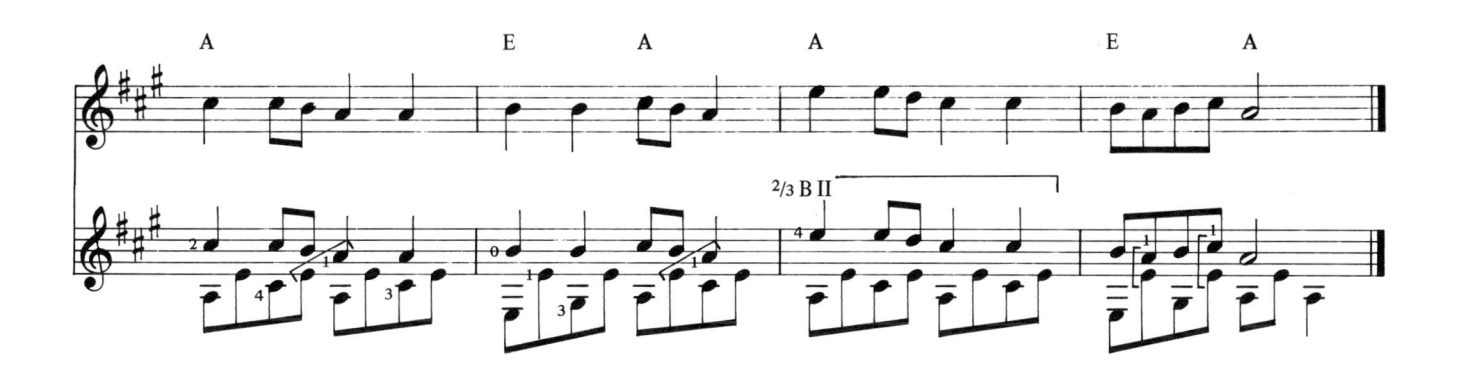

O Come, Little Children

Folk Song

May Song

Folk Song

Allegro moderato

Long, Long Ago

T. H. Bayly

Moderato

Allegro

S. Suzuki

Minuet 1

J.S. Bach

G/B D7/A G D G D G
G D G C G/B Am/C D D7 G
Em B7 Em Em B7 Em B7 Em
D7/A Em B7 Em G/B C Am D
D G D7 G D G D G
G D G C G/B Am/C D D7 G

Minuet 3

J.S. Bach

Chorus from "Judas Maccabaeus"

G. F. Handel

Maestoso

Gavotte

F. J. Gossec

Musette
Gavotte II from English Suite No. 3

J. S. Bach

*Note to Guitar: Play at V throughout.

Waltz
Op. 39, No. 15

J. Brahms

19

Theme from "Witches' Dance"

N. Paganini

21

Minuet in G

L. van Beethoven

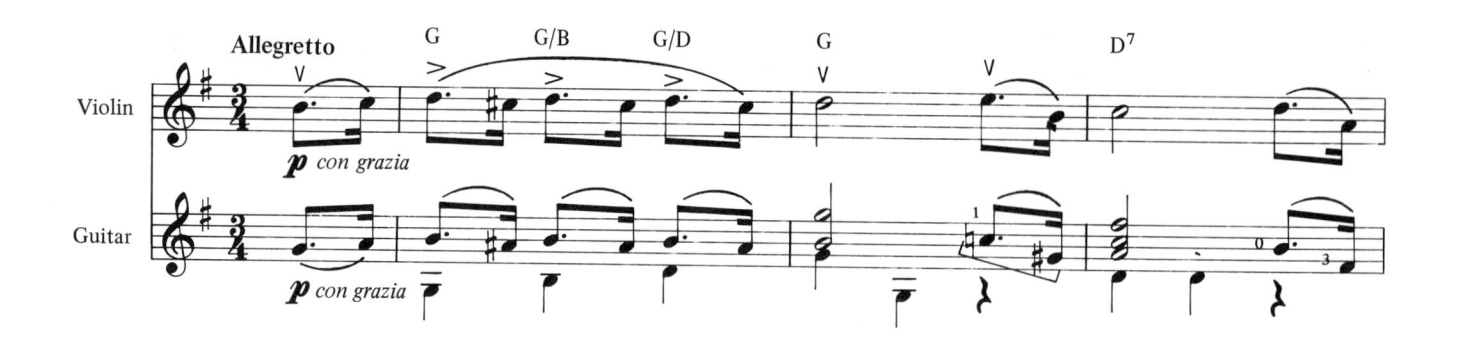

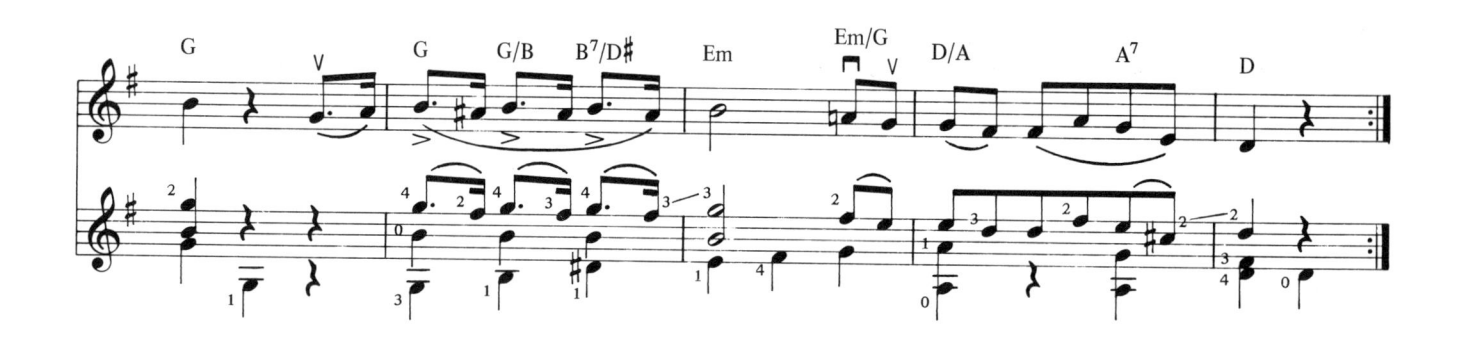

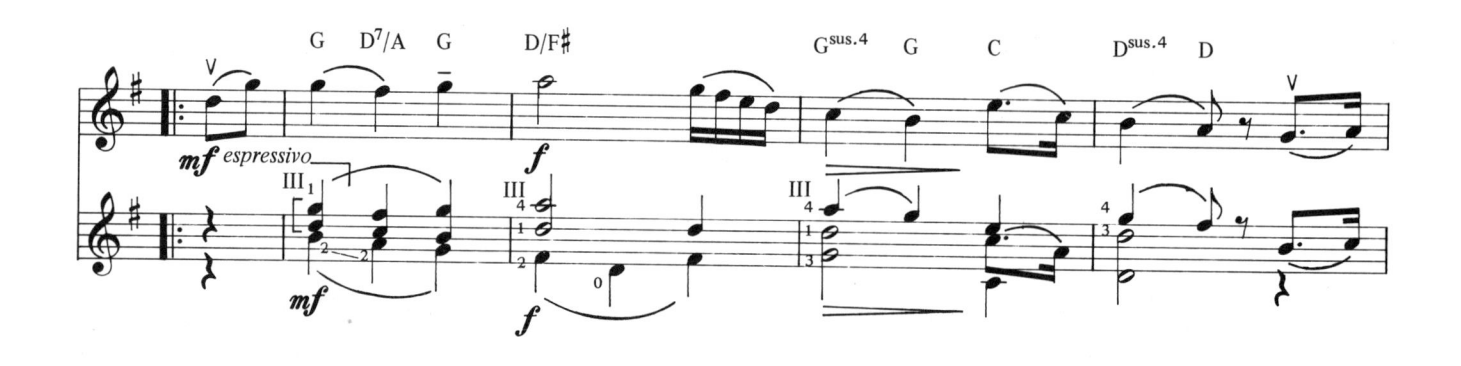

23

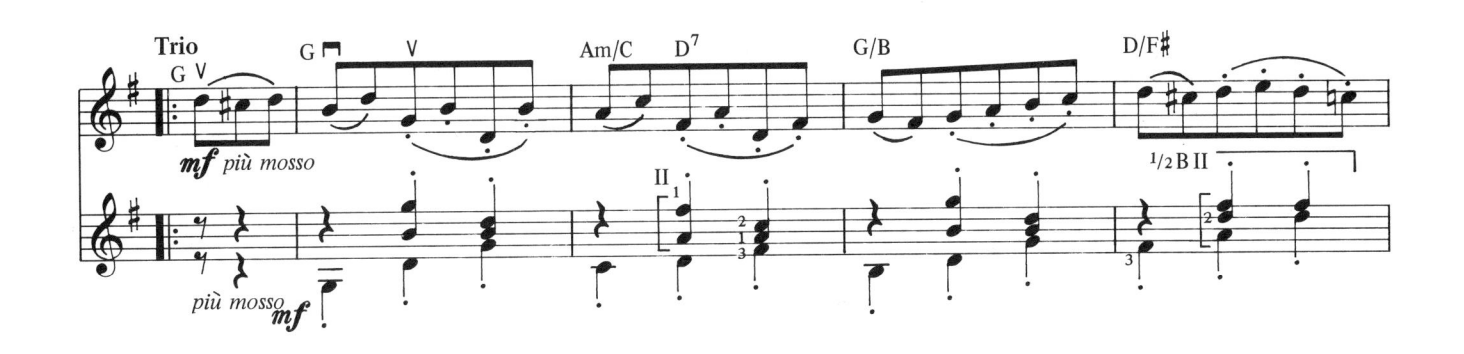

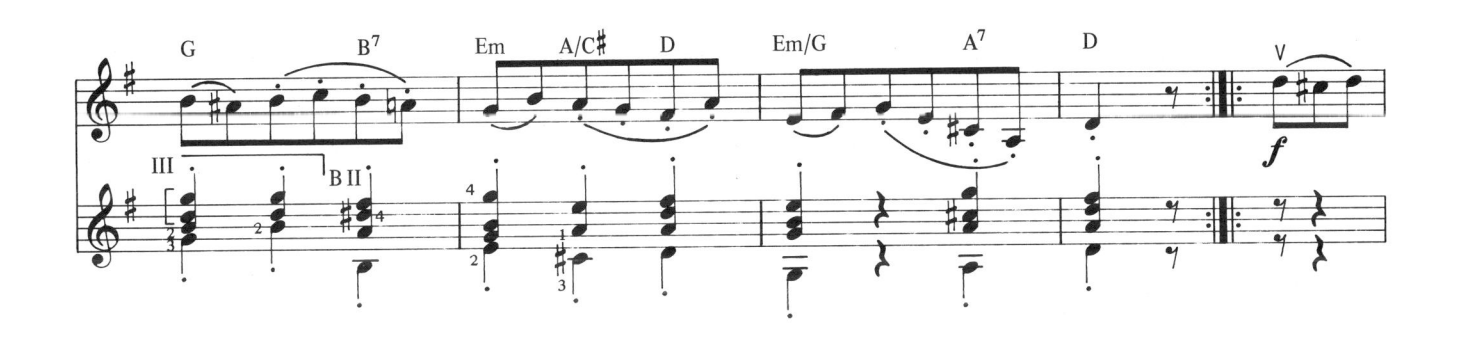

Minuet

L. Boccherini

25

Humoresque
Op. 101, No. 7

A. Dvořák

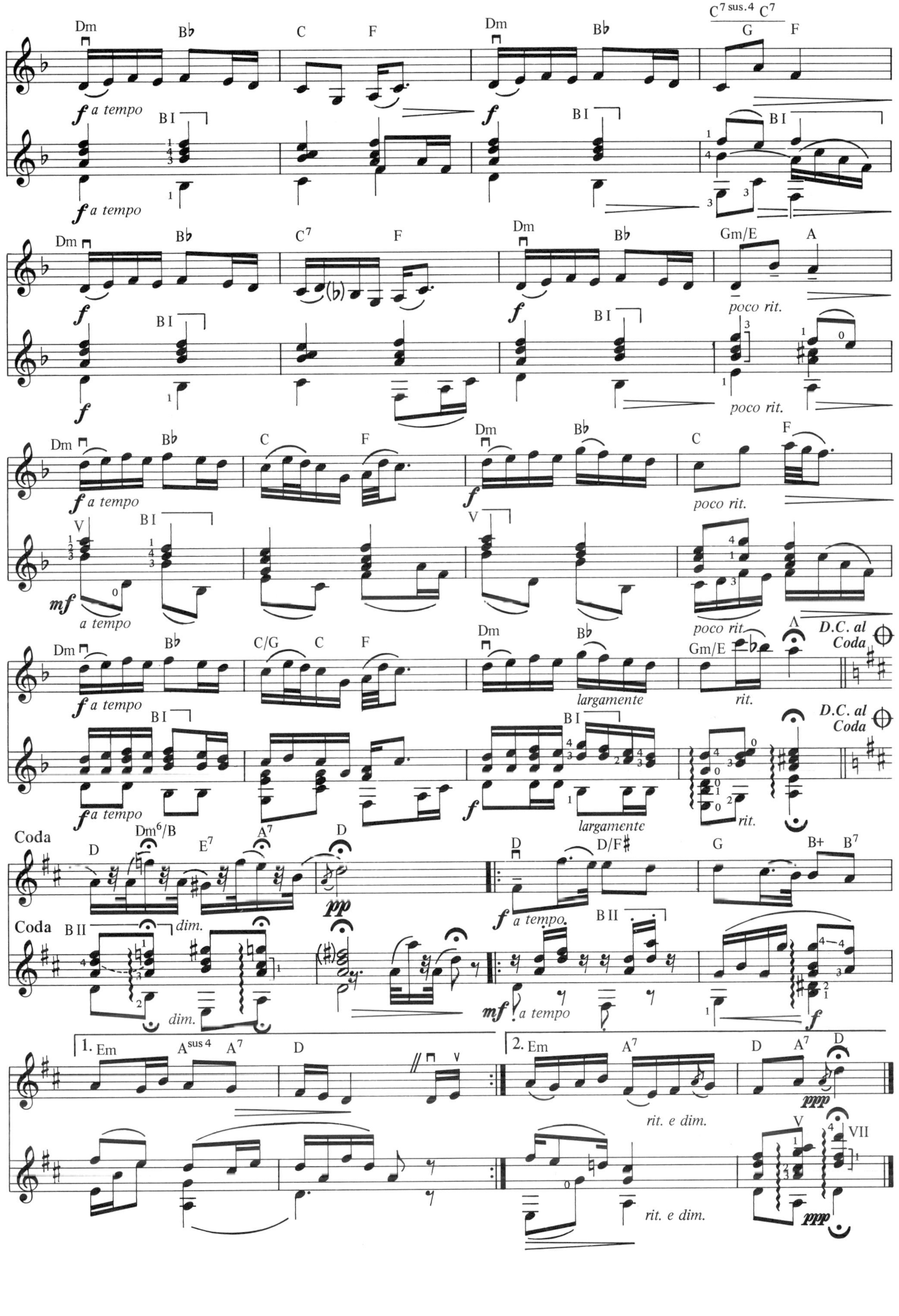
a tempo
poco rit.
largamente
rit.
D.C. al Coda
Coda
dim.
rit. e dim.

Gavotte

P. Martini

29

D
D
D
D
G
G
G
D
A7
D
Tacet
G
G
G
D
G
G
G
D7
G
Tacet
D
D
D
A7/D
D
Tacet
Bm
Bm
Bm/F#
F#7
Bm
Tacet
BII

31

Gavotte in D major

J.S. Bach

33

Minuet

J.S. Bach

Allegretto

35

Gm Dm E♭ maj.7 Cm/E♭ D D Cm F B♭ E♭ maj.7/G
Em Bm C Am B B Am D G C/E
D7/A D/F♯ Gm D Gm Dm E♭ maj.7 Cm/E♭ D D
B7 Em B Em Bm C Am B
G7/B G7 Cm F/A B♭ E♭ F B♭ B♭ F/A F
rinf.
E7 E7 Am D G C D G G D
rinf.
C7 F F/A F E♭ B♭ Cm B♭/D E♭ F B♭
A7 D D C G Am G C D G

37